THE VICTORIAN AND EDWARDIAN
BORDERLAND
FROM RARE PHOTOGRAPHS

In the same series
Victorian and Edwardian Fife from Old Photographs

By the same authors

PETER ADAMSON
St Andrews by the Northern Sea

RAYMOND LAMONT-BROWN
History of St Marks Church, Dewsbury
A Book of Epitaphs
Clarinda
Doncaster Rural District
Letters on Demonology and Witchcraft by Sir Walter Scott
Robert Burns's Commonplace Book
A Book of Superstitions
A Book of Proverbs
A Book of Witchcraft
Charles Kirkpatrick Sharpe's Witchcraft in Scotland
Phantoms of the Sea
General Trade of Berwick-on-Tweed
Robert Burns's Tour of the Borders
The Magic Oracles of Japan
Robert Burns's Tour of the Highlands and Stirlingshire
A New Book of Epitaphs
A Casebook of Military Mystery
Epitaph Hunting
Growing Up with the Highland Clans
Scottish Epitaphs
Lothian and the Southeast Borders

THE VICTORIAN AND EDWARDIAN
BORDERLAND
FROM RARE PHOTOGRAPHS

RAYMOND LAMONT-BROWN

AND

PETER ADAMSON

FOREWORD

BY

THE RT. HON. THE LORD HOME OF THE HIRSEL K.T.

ALVIE PUBLICATIONS ST ANDREWS

Peter Adamson dedicates this book to Linda
Raymond Lamont-Brown dedicates this book to his dear friends
May and Bill Montgomery of Berwick-on-Tweed

First published in 1981 by
Alvie Publications
52 Buchanan Gardens
St Andrews KY16 9LX

ISBN 0 950620017

Printed in Scotland by
Spectrum Printing Company
Burlington Street, Edinburgh

Contents

ACKNOWLEDGEMENTS

The authors would like to express their gratitude and thanks particularly to Mr Ian Brown, at the Department of Environmental Services, Ettrick and Lauderdale District Council, for his unfailing advice, help and encouragement in the collection of the rare photographs herein, without which the book would not have been possible. Further, the authors would like to thank Dr. Michael Robson of the Museum, Wilton Lodge Park, Hawick, for his valuable assistance and support. For this book many people have given help both individually and as members of clubs and societies; they are too numerous to mention but are none the less sincerely thanked.

Photographic credits and sources
University of St Andrews, 1.
The Rt. Hon. The Lord Home of the Hirsel, K.T., 2, 3, 6, 7, 8, 9, 19, 23, 62, 106, 125, 126, 160, 161.
Miss M. Gordon, Lasswade, 4, 179.
Wilton Lodge Museum, Hawick, 5, 10, 16, 17, 36, 37, 39, 40, 42, 43, 45, 70, 72, 76, 78, 83, 84, 85, 86, 100, 101, 121, 122, 123, 124, 127, 128, 134, 135, 141, 144, 145, 150, 153, 162, 163.
Selkirkshire Antiquarian Society, 11, 12, 13, 14, 25, 32, 42, 49, 71, 72, 88, 89, 90, 159, 165.
Ettrick and Lauderdale District Council Museum Service, 15, 138, 143.
Mr James Bryce, Edinburgh, 18, 48, 53, 73, 93, 103, 105, 109, 112, 119, 173, 175,176.
Capt. The Hon. Gerald Maitland Carew, Thirlestane Castle, Lauder, 20, 21, 139.
Anstruther Fisheries Museum, 22, 54, 55, 57.
Borders Regional Library Service (Galashiels Library), 24, 46, 95.
Mr Ian Brown, Walkerburn, 74, 79, 80, 81, 99, 152, 168.
Mr John Rogerson, Galashiels, 47, 82.
Mr Jack Cruickshank, Selkirk, 87.
'William Renton Collection', via Rev. Hugh Mackay, Duns, 71, 97.
Mrs Anne Gordon, St Boswells, 33, 92, 178.
Old Gala Club, 94, 96, 97, 98, 142, 145, 146, 148, 155, 156, 166, 181.
Mr W.A. Montgomery, Berwick-on-Tweed, 104.
Dundee District Libraries, 107.
Hector Innes, A.I.I.P, photographer, Kelso, 110, 171.
Rev. James Brown, Kirk Yetholm, 183.
Mr & Mrs Tinline, Bellfield, Lilliesleaf, 113, 120.
Lt. Col & Mrs J.D.G. Lineham, Melrose, 34, 38, 64, 65, 114, 116, 169, 170.
National Museum of Antiquities of Scotland, Country Life Section (NMAS/CLS), 118.
Raymond Lamont-Brown, St Andrews, 129, 149.
Brian Holton, Gattonside, St Andrews, 41, 52, 130, 157.
Mr T. Swinton Purves, Galashiels, 44, 135, 136, 137, 177, 182.
Mr D.W. Veitch, Peebles, 35, 59, 63, 67, 131, 132, 158.
Mr Hutcheson, Melrose, 140.
Mrs Short, Galashiels (NMAS/CS), 26.
Mrs Anne Scott, Melrose (NMAS/CS), 27.
Mrs Patti Rae, via Gladstonecourt Museum Biggar (NMAS/CS), 28.
J.M.M. Scott, Morebattle, Roxburghshire, 30, 66.
Col. W.H. Oliver, Blainslie, Galashiels, 31.
Mr L.B. Smith, 29, 58.
Messrs C.H. Dexter Corporation, Chirnside Bridge Papermill, 51.
Mr. T.D. Purves, Gavinton, Berwickshire, 60.
Miss M. Dagg, Newcastleton (NMAS/CLS), 61.
Mr W.R.B. Whitie, Peebles, 154.
Mr Richard Dawson, Seahouses, Northumberland, 36.
Mr Bob Mason, Jedburgh, 147, 151, 173, 183.
Mrs J. Hart, Melrose, 172.

The Acknowledgements herein, in themselves, constitute a useful research tool as to where quality collections are housed.
RAYMOND LAMONT-BROWN, and PETER ADAMSON.

FOREWORD

By The Right Hon. The Lord Home of the Hirsel, K.T.

THE Border country has changed less than many other places in Britain in the last 100 years. The Tweed dominates its valley; agriculture and textiles are still the basic industries; the Abbeys stand as a reminder of early Christianity, and the people go about their tasks in comparative order and peace.

But it only needs the photographs in this book to illustrate the contrasts between now and then. The dress, the transport and the tools of the trade all speak of an era where the pace of life was much slower than that of today, and where the individual workman had only recently begun to be replaced by the machine.

The pictures of the penny-farthings at Yarrow; the yarn drays at Hawick; and the clothes of the cricketers at Selkirk will seem quite unreal to the young generation of today—so fast does time fly.

Queen Victoria, when she came for her short visit to the Borders, will have seen people working for long hours and for wages which would seem pitifully small in comparison with today. But she had started her reign in a deep recession, and when she stayed in Kelso in 1867 the country was beginning to pull out of it. So, while she would have seen hardship and want, she would have detected an underlying buoyancy and confidence that Britain was on the make. In fact, within a few years, the people in the photographs in the book saw a Britain which was the workshop of the world, and in that prosperity the Borders shared.

Let us hope that the photographers and writers of 100 years on will be able to read and record that modern history has repeated itself in progress and recovery.

'Is there room for me?' Kelso Abbey, c 1880.

INTRODUCING
THE VICTORIAN AND EDWARDIAN BORDERLAND

QUEEN Victoria made her first official visit to the Scottish Borders in 1867, twenty-five years after she had made her initial sojourn to Scotland accompanied by her consort Prince Albert of Saxe-Coburg-Gotha. From Carlisle she travelled to Hawick with a retinue of her own children, governesses and courtiers led by Sir Thomas Biddulph, Keeper of the Privy Purse and her celebrated physician, Sir William Jenner. Her presence stimulated great interest among the folk of Teviotdale, who requested that her progress be slow so that as many people as possible could see her.

In her *Leaves From The Journal Of Our Life in the Highlands,* under the date Wednesday August 21, 1867, she wrote: '. . . we entered Teviotdale and descended it, entering the valley of the Tweed at St Boswell's. Between St. Boswell's and Kelso, at Roxburgh station, we crossed the Teviot again. We passed close under the Eildon Hills, three high points rising from the background. The country is extremely picturesque, valleys with fine trees and streams, intermingled with great cultivation. Only after half-past eleven did we reach Kelso station, which was very prettily decorated, and where were standing the Duke and Duchess of Roxburghe, Lord Bowmont, the Duke of Buccleuch, and Lord C. Ker, as well as General Hamilton, commanding the forces in Scotland'.

The Queen stayed at Sir John Vanburgh's stately mansion of Floors Castle, the home of Sir James Innes-Ker, the 6th Duke of Roxburghe and his wife Susanna Stephenia. Victoria's memories of Kelso were vivid. She wrote: 'The little town of Kelso is very picturesque, and there were triumphal arches, and no end of pretty mottoes, and every house was decorated with flowers and flags. Fifty ladies dressed in white strewed flowers as we passed. Volunteers were out and bands played. At the Market Place the carriage stopped; an address was presented, not read; and a little girl was held up to give me an enormous bouquet. Immense and most enthusiastic cheering. We then drove on, amidst continued crowds and hearty cheers, up to the very park gates, where the old Sheriff, eighty-five years old, was presented'.

While here Victoria visited St Boswells, Ravenswood (Old Melrose), and Melrose, and saw Dryburgh Abbey and Galashiels at a distance. At Sir Walter Scott's old home, Abbotsford, she was greeted by James Robert Hope-Scott (who had married Sir Walter's grand-daughter, Charlotte Lockhart) and his second wife Lady Victoria Fitzalan Howard (Victoria's god-daughter). At Leaderfoot Bridge she inspected the Berwickshire Volunteers (commanded by the Earl of Haddington's son, Lord Binning). She went on to Jedburgh and had a trip into Berwickshire; the Queen described the Merse (the old name for the richest tract of agricultural land in Scotland, held for the King of Scots by the Earls of March) as 'very pretty, hilly, wooded and cultivated'. On Saturday, August 24, she left Floors for Edinburgh, and never returned to the Borders for a protracted visit.

Victoria had, of course, visited Berwick-on-Tweed when she opened Robert Stephenson's Royal Border Bridge on August 28, 1850. Berwick station was built on the site of the medieval castle by the North British Railway Co in 1844-46 to link their rails with those of the York, Newcastle and Berwick Railway. Victoria's visit lasted twelve minutes! Incidentally, Berwick-on-Tweed, the southeast gateway to the Borders, saw many changes in Victoria and Edward's days. With the opening of the Royal Border Bridge spanning the Tweed, the Edinburgh to London line was complete and the town harbour lost much of its former trade, but the fishing fleet continued to flourish. The famous Berwick smacks carried goods and passengers between Leith, Berwick and London well into Victoria's reign.

Across the Tweed, Tweedmouth and Spittal were then parts of the old Borough of Berwick-on-Tweed, here a new dock was built 1872-77 to accommodate the larger vessels which dealt with Border grain and timber. Because of its port, Berwick did not suffer the ravages of the Civil wars of the 17th century and the 18th century decline which so fettered Border trade; and although the railway did take away trade, by the mid-years of Victoria's reign the town boasted a good diversity of commerce. For instance, Messrs James R. Black & Co Ltd, were agents for Border Corn Seed and Oilcake in the busy years of 1868-1886. Border thirst was slaked by the Border Brewery Co in its expanded works of 1887, and all over the Borders the boilers of George Black of Tweedmouth powered farm and factory. Berwick's thoroughfares were thronged on market days in Victoria and Edward's days with Borderers stocking up with necessities, from the draperies of Messrs Paxton and Purves (1802) to John Wilson's ironmongery (1848) and from the agricultural chemicals supplied by John Elliot (1844) to the confectionery of S.E. Simpson (1852).

Easy as it was for her Borderers to classify their age as Victorian, the cheering crowds when she appeared were unable to typecast the person of Victoria. Her tendencies tied her to no race. No stratum of Border society could claim her. She bestowed her friendships on the individual, whether Master of the Berwickshire hunt, or porridge-fed chiel from Gala. 'She is religious', said the minister of Kelso, yet, in reality, she accepted theologically only what she wished. Those around her expected her to admonish God in the same vein as she would an erring lady-in-waiting. As she smiled and waved to her Borderers, she did it unwillingly—not because she disliked them, but because she preferred the land they lived in to their physical company. At once a recluse and a gregarious friend, confident in herself yet near to swooning at the opening of Parliament, unaccountably and entirely unpredictable, the Victoria the Borderers saw was a complete enigma.

Victoria knew the Scottish middle-class in general and the Border lairds in particular, fairly well; her daughter Princess Louise, after all, was to marry a future Duke of Argyll. Yet, Border fashion did not ape the Queen. By her sixtieth year of rule the left-over Regency school of social mores had been swept away. The fashionable looked to the Queen's youngest daughter, Princess Beatrice, last child, and constant companion, as an example. Houses rang to 'The Beatrice Walze'; for in Border parlours the piano had become the status symbol of the age.

The Borderland as Victoria saw it was a distinct geographical unit: Berwickshire, Roxburgh, Selkirk and Peebles were isolated to some extent from the rest of Scotland by the Tweed basin. For centuries the Lammermuirs, the Moorfoots and the Pentlands had bred parochialism, even though this land had felt the brunt of English rapaciousness. The Cheviots, too, added a border bastion to the coastal plain from St Abbs to Seahouses; which in itself tended to contain local culture. In Victorian and Edwardian times, for instance, the English town (firmly so only since 1603) of Berwick-on-Tweed, owed more to Border Scottish culture than to surrounding Northumberland (or North Durham as this area was formerly known). Neither wholly Scottish or English, Berwick retained a certain independence which is recognised in a curious legal story. Because of the town's peculiar position, Berwick was invariable mentioned in Acts of Parliament as remembered in the old jingle:

1.   H.M. Queen Victoria, circa 1890.

They talk of England and Scotland indeed,
'Tis Great Britain and Ireland and Berwick-on-Tweed!

This is the basic reason for the tale that Berwick remained at War with Czarist Russia; for it is said that the town was included specifically in the declaration of hostilities on the outbreak of the Crimean War in 1854, but was omitted from the treaty of peace in 1856!

A sober morality founded on the gospel of self-help and a reverence for the domestic virtues, were the hallmarks of the middle-class Borderer of Victoria's reign. By the time Edward came to the throne in 1901, however, they had become increasingly conscious of social divisions and they found great satisfaction in their corporate identity.

Most of the heavy industry of the Borderland was situated in the west. Galashiels on the Gala Water, described by Dorothy Wordsworth in 1803 as 'the village of Galashiels pleasantly situated on the banks of the stream', was the chief centre for tweed manufacture in Scotland. The designation 'tweed' had nothing to do with the River Tweed. It derives from a clerical error. An English clerk wrote the Scots word *tweels*, meaning woollen fabric, as 'tweeds', and the name has stuck ever since. Galashiels was also known for its tanneries and dyeworks. By Victoria's day the production of 'Galashiels Grey', a coarse woollen cloth had died out. Yet, Sir Walter Scott and his friends saved the day by sporting a fashion for the small black and white 'Shepherd's Check'. Previously used for shawls and shepherd's plaids, the check and tartan kept the mills busy up to the 1900s. Galashiels was always in the forefront of the fight against declining markets. Its tenacity led to the founding of the Scottish College of Textiles in the town in 1909.

11

Centred on its market cross, rebuilt in 1898, Selkirk retained its reputation for weaving in Victoria and Edward's days. There had been Incorporated Weavers here since 1608, and the early 19th century saw the growth of tweed mills below the town on the south bank of the Ettrick Water; among them Ettrick Mill, Yarrow Mill and Linglie Mill were prominent. On the right of the modern Post Office building is the place where Robbie Douglas opened his bakery in 1859. Here he made the famous 'Selkirk bannock', a round yeasted fruit loaf which is now famous the world over. Douglas insisted on exactly the right ingredients for his bannocks (butter from the pastures of Ettrick, and sultanas only from Turkey); if there were no such ingredients available, no bannocks were made. When she visited Abbotsford in 1867, Victoria refused the cold collation and chose instead from slices of the bannocks.

Hawick, a town which figured often and prominently in the events of Border warfare and forays had had its hosiery trade established in 1771 by Bailie John Hardy. Although a depressed industry by 1860, the hosiery (combined with tweeds as in the case of Wiliam Laidlaw & Sons) did provide work. The hours were long (6am to 8pm) and the pay was meagre; in Victoria's day a child of 11 earned 3/- to 4/- (15-20 pence) per week.

The only royal burgh in Berwickshire, Lauder, was an important coaching stop-off in Victorian days. As many as six coaches passed either way daily and once there was at least twenty inns in the pint-sized, but typical Border town. In the 18th century Innerleithen was famous for its woollen industry started by Alexander Brodie, but in Victorian times Innerleithen's reputation increased as a spa. Victorians flocked to the pumps to benefit from the mineral waters. Here the blue and white pump-room, erected in 1826 by the Earl of Traquair, was reconstructed in 1896; behind it was St Ronan's Well, the name of the novel by Sir Walter Scott which brought many Victorians here on solemn pilgrimage.

Despite pockets of industrialisation, then, the Victorian and Edwardian Borderer was predominantly sheep-grain-cattle-fish orientated. Eyemouth and St Abbs were notable fishing harbours and grain mills were scattered throughout the Borderland. The economic fortunes of the southeast Borders were very much tied-in with the fishing trade. Eyemouth was the chief town of the Borderland fishing district which extended from St Abbs in Berwickshire, to Amble in Northumberland. In 1894, 451 boats were working this strip. Fortunes varied by catch from the depression of Victoria's early years to the phenomenal catches of 1883. The white fish industry was the recognised trade of the coast and from 1880 to 1900 the North Sea was a 'veritable mine of wealth'. Often the toll was high. Eyemouth suffered the worst disaster in the Border area in Victorian and Edwardian times. On Friday, October 14, 1881, a fishing fleet was destroyed off Eyemouth with the loss of 189 lives.

The southern Borderers were much concerned with trade with England, mostly through Berwick-on-Tweed. In the rural economy, Border villages remained self-sufficient until Edward's death in 1910 and craftsmen were basically mainly associated with agricultural life.

By Gladstone's Reform Act of 1884-85, the Borderers had manhood suffrage, and remained overwhelmingly Liberal; although from the Earl of Rosebery's government of 1894 the Liberals were in opposition until 1905. One reason why the Gladstonian Liberals were so popular in the Borders, was that they were deemed to stand for 'moral principle', which tied-in very well with the Border triple ethic of Temperance-Calvinism and Independence.

Overall, Border family life throughout Victoria's reign, and for a large part of Edward's, centred on the church. The kirk scene in Victorian Scotland had undoubtedly been dominated by the Disruption of 1843. At this time some 500 kirk ministers had left the 'established' Church of Scotland because they insisted on the right of each presbytery to veto the appointment of a minister whom it considered unsuitable. These dissidents formed the Free Church of Scotland. The United Presbyterian Church had been formed by an earlier secession. An amalgamation took place in 1900 to form the United Free Church.

The presbyterian Church of Scotland went through a number of doctrinal and organisational controversies, but during 1837-1910, the Church of Scotland retained a much greater hold over Scots Borderers, than did the Church of England, or the Nonconformists of the 'English side'. In 1902, 10—15 percent of the Border population still went to church regularly. A Border minister was a man of some social consequence (with the schoolmaster, provost, bailies and the local doctor), having a hand in matters spiritual and temporal. He was expected to be welfare officer, kirkyard arbiter, marriage guidance counsellor and children's officer, as well as shepherding souls towards the great hereafter.

In Victoria and Edward's Borderland, Sunday was a sterile day of well-worn ritual. Families and servants (the latter usually taking turns as duties permitted) repaired to church. All were dressed in decorous greys and blacks, with the occasional child breaking the leaden fashion with a kilt.

The street scenes of the large Border towns of Victoria and Edward's days reflected the clutter of the average home. People went out from the early hours, the first afoot being the milk vendors and the bakers with their baskets of steaming baps, scones and pancakes. By 8 o'clock the itinerants were out: The 'ingan johnnies', the knife-grinders, the pan menders and the home-produce sellers. It was a scene of noise with the wheels and horses of drays, carriages and carts being the noisiest. Busy, perhaps, but wages were low and distress was only too apparent; the extent was to be brought into focus by Conservative Prime Minister A.J. Balfour's Royal Commission on the Poor Law and the Relief of Distress.

Half the houses in the Borders had only one or two rooms by Edward's day and overcrowding was a constant hardship. A typical industrial worker's dwelling was that provided in 1842 for the papermill workers at Chirnside Bridge, Berwickshire. They were described by the *Berwick Warder* newspaper as occupying 'a pretty steep bank . . . The cottages are all of two storeys. They make in all 22 dwelling-houses; four families entering at one door in the centre houses — and two in the end ones. Each family has two rooms — the outer one of which in the upstairs dwelling . . . containing two box-beds — and the inner a tent-bed with curtains. Each room is lighted by one window. The work people seemed to approve very much of the accommodation afforded them'.

Much of the Border workingclass accommodation was insanitary and poorly designed with rents ranging from 1/- to 1/6 (5—7½ pence). Generally speaking the rents were reasonable in relation to workers' wages; but with no room for extravagant frivolities such as an over-indulgence in soap.

Border wage rates were pretty low as a predominantly rural community: For agricultural workers were, in the main, lower paid than industrial. In 1902 the average agricultural wage had risen to 19/- (95 pence) a week. Agricultural workers were able to eke out a much better diet than the industrial workers with their 'perks' of vegetables and animal produce. Agriculture did recover after 1900 helped by the wider acceptance of such systems as Robert H. Elliott's ley-farming, evolved at Clifton Park, Roxburgh, in the 1880s. From 1890-1910 the development of poultry-farming, fruit-growing and market gardening was increased leading to a more healthy rural budget.

In spite of the fact that Scotland was linked with England in constitutional development, in economic expansion and growing social conscience, Scotland retained her national identity in

Victorian and Edwardian times—and the Borderers their individuality. Border farmers were more progressive than in England and were keen Free Traders, although they concerned themselves little with foreign affairs.

At this time Scotland had her own land laws, her judicial organisation, to some extent her old electoral and education systems, so by and large the Borderers were better read than those on 'the English side'. English visitors, in fact, found the Borderers 'surprisingly well-informed'.

The administration of Border burghs was modernised in William IV's reign by the Scottish Municipal Reform Act (1833); the Burgh Police Act of 1892 consolidated all previous legislation. County councils in the Borders had been set up under terms of the Local Government (Scotland) Act of 1889 and the whole pattern of Border municipal life was completed by the Local Government (Scotland) Act of 1894. The latter exhorted that parish councils be elected to replace the parochial boards which administered the Poor Law. Thus was the Borders given a democratic (if somewhat parish-pump at times!) government at grass-roots level. On the English side there were corresponding Acts.

Although the Poor Law (Scotland) Act 1845 made it so that each parish was no longer responsible for its own poor, and established Inspectors of the Poor and Workhouses, it is important to realise that welfare care in the Borders was largely provided by philanthropic individuals until 1914. School meals and books, for instance, were usually provided by local lairds. A 'soup kitchen' was provided by local farmers at Edrom (Berwickshire) up to 1914. All that was required in return was 'gratitude'; the children of Allanton (Berwickshire) school were admonished by the local laird (Sir George Houston-Boswall) for booing the Tory candidate (the laird's choice) at one election—Sir George had bought the school-books!

In the Education (Scotland) Act of 1872 (English equivalent 1870), the state for the first time accepted direct responsibility for educating Border children. Even so the administrators of the Act retained the duty of electing school boards within parish and burgh schools. By 1902, 85 percent of Border children were attending schools regularly. In 1890 elementary education in the Borders was virtually free, although fees continued to be charged for secondary education. Wider powers were given to school boards in 1908 when another Education (Scotland) Act was passed. Now the boards had a hand in medical examination and supervision of health in schools, and education for the 5—14 year olds was compulsory.

Schools of note, of course, had been established in the Borders for centuries. For instance, Kelso Grammar School had developed from a monastic seminary to a flourishing secondary school by 1669.

The Borders were to be represented in the development of photography.

Two years after Queen Victoria came to the throne on June 20, 1837, practical methods of photography were announced. Although a French invention—Joseph Nicéphore Niepce (1765-1832) took what is generally considered to be the first photograph—photography was first popularised in an amateur way in Scotland. With the active support of the Jedburgh-born scientist Sir David Brewster (1781-1868), Principal of the United College, St Andrews University, the inventor William Henry Fox Talbot (1800-77) sought to develop his original photographic research. Fox Talbot developed in 1840 a way to record likenesses—the calotype. He patented his invention in 1841 as the 'talbotype', and was anxious that his system be popularised. Fox Talbot wished for the recognition which had been given to the Frenchman Louis Jacques Mandé Daguerre (1789-1851), whose pictures on an iodised plate (daguerréotypes) had won him international fame. Scotland was not hampered by the strict patent restrictions upon inventions and Fox Talbot wanted to corner the market. So with the help of Brewster and others, like Dr John Adamson (1809-70), Fox Talbot's invention was secured and launched as an art form. The Borders were to have a definite link in the development of photography in Scotland, for some of Fox Talbot's early exposures were of Border landscapes (See page 18).

From 1843 to 1878 photography was very much the work of academic dabblers. It was too expensive a process for the general hobbyist. There were, of course, 'itinerant photographers' who came to the Borders, took rooms in a hotel and advertised in the papers for local custom. Their photographs were mostly vapid poses and generally this was a summer occupation. But the development of photography in Scotland caught the imagination of many in the Borders, spurred on by the famous landscape painter David Octavius Hill (1802-70) and the distinguished commercial photographer Thomas Annan.

Following the inventions of such as Richard Leach Maddox, by 1878 the amateur could buy photographic material without employing the tedious skilled process of making each chemical. In 1888 George Eastman of New York patented the first box camera. This transformed the practice of photography and thousands of ordinary folk were able to develop the pastime.

The structure of non-sporting entertainment in the Borders during 1837-1910 was very much by social class. Entertainment was usually restricted by cash available so leisure time was taken up by self-improvement and self-amusement. Artistic diversions were still home-made and no self-respecting damsel of good voice ever visited without taking her music in her reticule. Reading flourished and from the 1860s every major town in the Borders had its own public library. It was the age too, of the 'learned society'. The Hawick Archaeological Society was founded in 1856 and all the major towns followed suit with Literary, Eclectic and Winter Lecture Clubs.

Charles Dickens brought 'live readings' to the Borders when he performed at Berwick-on-Tweed in 1858 and 1861. Scott was devoured *ad nauseam*, and by the 1890s new writers fought for prominence. Young Kipling's Indian tales vied with the Celtic voice of Yeats, and Arnold Bennett, still chained to ladies' journals, jockeyed with doom-laded H.G. Wells for reader time. Prominent too, were the 'kailyarders', Ian Maclaren (John Watson), S.R. Crockett and J.M. Barrie; but Border hearts beat proudly to read the works of Andrew Lang, born in 1844 at Viewfields, Selkirk.

Extravagances of the 'Naughty Nineties' did not have much effect on the Borders, for the bucks who could afford the adultery of high society went outside the county boundaries to indulge. Opera and concerts too, mainly had to be visited outside the Borderlands, but school bands and travelling players introduced music to the lower orders. Amateur concerts were popular in Border villages drawing upon local 'talent'; occasionally a circus would appear bringing wonderment and mystery to the unsophisticated Borderer.

Eating out became the rage of the middle classes from the 1890s and ladies of good reputation could at last sup in public. It was the age of the hostess, with lavish dinner parties. In the 1906 edition of Mrs Beeton's *Book of Household Management* the Border hostess was advised to produce this 'simple' breakfast for her shooting or cycling parties:

Oatmeal Porridge
Kidney Omelet
Baked eggs (au gratin)
Fried Cod

Grilled Ham
Potted Game
Veal Cake
Stewed Prunes and Cream
Scones, Rolls, Toast, Bread
Butter, Marmalade, Jam
Tea, Coffee, Milk

The lower classes were lucky to afford the first item as their breakfast.

Whist drives became a craze in 1909 and led to many marriages, or so according to a local report—'but for whist many girls who have little opportunity of meeting the opposite sex would remain spinsters!' So many a Border lass looked to have her ace trumped on a Saturday night.

Yet cards and books, eating out and concerts were mainly a middle class entertainment. Many workingclass folk still sought solace from life in alcohol. A sad social comment comes from many a faded photograph: For, under the provisions of the Children Act of 1909, no child was allowed into a bar where alcoholic drink was consumed—so hoards of children are to be seen outside pubs awaiting the coming of their fathers (usually to guide their faltering footsteps home). It was not considered decorous for a woman, of any class, to be seen in a pub: Those who did frequent hostelries were deemed 'no better than they ought to be'.

In 1897 the Borders shared in Britain's indulgence in an orgy of patriotic pride at the Queen's Diamond Jubilee. Yet, already there loomed on the horizon the problems which divided Britain in the early years of the 20th century, from women's suffrage to the struggle for fair wages and fair prices: Problems which were to spill over into Edward VII's reign. Edwardian Scotland was discontented and violent. Pratically in the Borders was seen the extremes of wealth and poverty, but there was little of the radical change, or conservative reaction of the big cities.

At 6.30 pm on Tuesday, January 22, 1901, Queen Victoria drew her last breath at Osborne House, Isle of Wight, in the arms of her grandson, William II of Germany, 'Kaiser Bill' of World War I. Although 82, Queen Victoria's days had been chipped away by rheumatism, eye disease and aphasis. She had reigned for 64 years, longer than any other British sovereign. At last Edward came into his inheritance and a new age had dawned.

'Edwardian' is undoubtedly a description that suggests largesse and leisure, yet the King who left his name on an era only reigned for ten years, after Victoria's death. Although the Edwardian age was brief, it remains more in nostalgic memory than Victoria's because of the opulence and elegance of its monarch.

Even though after the death of the Prince Consort in 1861, Victoria refused to discharge most of the ceremonial and diplomatic duties of her office, Edward, Prince of Wales, was less wellknown as a monarch in the Borders than his mother. Edward VII was 60 by the time he came to the throne and his mother, afraid that he was to go the way of her 'wicked uncles', had denied her son any administrative power: Consequently he knew little about his Borderlands.

Indeed Edward had an ambivalent image in the Borders. There were those of the middle and upper middle class who saw him as a paternal, jovial and energetic; and there were those of the lower orders who had fellow-feeling for the King's delight in race horses. The King was never more popular amongst the Border labourers than when his horses won (particulary when his

2. H.R.H. Albert Edward, Prince of Wales, around his twenty-first birthday in 1862.

horse *Minoru* won the Derby in 1909). But the Sunday black-coated Border Calvinists saw Edward as gluttonous, lecherous, limited in intelligence, self-indulgent, pompous and irritable. They had been happier with the sombre, straight-laced reign of his mother. Most Border mantlepieces bore above it a picture of the 'Auld Queen'—few sported likenesses of her son.

The real Edward, fat on six lavish meals a day, was restless in spirit and always in need of entertainment. He was an extrovert, fond of pretty, vivacious women and bored by academics. Yet, he was fastidious in correct court etiquette, a marked contrast to his morality.

The King's choice of name was to cause some controversy in the Borders. He resolved to be called Edward, contrary to Victoria's expressed wishes that the use of any name but her husband's 'would be monstrous'. No Edward had ever reigned in Scotland, and race memories of the first three English Kings called Edward, caused anguish in some Border hearts. Border sympathisers with the Scottish Patriotic Association made noisy complaint in Hawick and Galashiels, but were whisked away between burly constables. Several Church of Scotland ministers deliberately missed out Edward's ordinal number from the loyal address read in churches.

Even so, as a royal personage, Edward enjoyed a popularity unknown to any English monarch since the years immediately following Charles II's restoration in 1660.

Edward VII made no official visit to the Borders, though he made a royal progress to Scotland in the year of his Coronation. The nearest he came to the Borders was when he ended his 1902 tour as the guest of the Prince and Princess Edward of Saxe-Weimar at North Berwick. He called on the Conservative Prime Minister A.J. Balfour at Wittingehame,

17

and then took tea at Tyninghame with the Earl of Haddington. Nevertheless a Border laird or two had an eye on Edward when they made additions to their property; some making sure that they would have enough accommodation for HRH should he care to call. One such was Sir Hubert Jerningham (1842-1914), Liberal MP for Berwick Borough 1887-1910, when he built Longridge Towers in 1878. Edward disappointed them all!

The Edwardian Age came to an end on May 6, 1910, when Edward VII died at Buckingham Place. With the king's passing an era went into decline to slip away into the costliest conflict the world has ever known in 1914. The kingdom which was Edward VII's legacy to his son George V was soon to be riven with industrial and civil discontent. Wage rates had hardly improved in the ten years of Edward's reign; and the divisive display of wealth and extravagance which had characterised Edward's lifestyle left the lower classes dissatisfied and resentful.

Yet in the 73 years covered by this book the spread of popular education, the increased mobility of its inhabitants, the rise of trade unionism had made more changes to the life styles of the people than the previous 100 years.

This book is concerned with showing some of the social changes in the Borderland 1837 to 1910. Herein is a distillation of Victorian and Edwardian characteristics and moods as seen by the camera, which became an indispensable modern recorder of social history.

RAYMOND LAMONT-BROWN

3.   Abbotsford, the house built by Sir Walter Scott and in which he lived from 1812-1832, photographed by William Henry Fox Talbot, circa 1840.

CHAPTER ONE

THE FACE OF THE BORDERS

5. Thomas Gray (1856-1910), manufacturer of gingham—a cotton fabric originally manufactured in India. Gray, who lived in Earlston, was a wellknown Border fiddler.

6, & 7. Grandfather and grandson. Charles Alexander Douglas-Home (1834-1919) was the 12th Earl of Home; picture taken in 1877.
Alexander Frederick Douglas-Home, taken at Springhilll, 1909, when he was six years old, and the only time he ever donned the kilt! The boy went on to become the 14th Earl of Home and disclaimed the 1605 title in 1963; he was Prime Minister 1963-64, and was created a Life Baron in 1974.

8. The present Lord Home of the
    Hirsel's brother and sister: The Hon.
    Henry Montagu (aged 2) and Lady
    Bridget (aged 4) at Bamburgh Beach,
    Northumberland, 1909.
    A fine example of Edwardian
    children's beach wear.

9. A ladder of Douglas-Homes! Issobel, Margaret
    and Beatie cascade behind the stylish
    Miss Elphinstone: at their feet is 'Charlie'
    (1873-1951), Charles Cospatrick Archibald,
    the 13th Earl of Home.

10. The Common Riding Fife & Drum Band, Hawick, 1907. Few men of the era were totally clean-shaven

11. Kinderspiel held in the Lawson Memorial Church Hall, Selkirk, to celebrate the Coronation of George V, 1911. The Organist was John Dickson.

12. Andrew Lang
    (1844-1912), born at
    Viewfield, Selkirk, became
    famous for his 'Fairy
    Books' titled by colour.
    Poet, historian and scholar
    he spent much time in St
    Andrews where he is
    buried.

13. T. McGlory,
    J. Mathieson and
    W. Douglas, the
    Burgh Officer, who
    'Cried the Burley' at
    the Selkirk Common
    Riding. This was the
    proclaiming of the
    list of the principal
    riders; and the
    'Burleymen'
    examined annually
    the boundaries of the
    town land for unlawful
    encroachments.

14. Bell Spence of Back Row, Selkirk.

15. Albert Wallace, 'The Border Minstrel', Selkirk.

16. Robert Laidlaw Brown, known as 'Magenta Bob', d 1900, Hawick.

17. Little Aggie, Hawick.

18. Isabella Richardson, whose world famous hostelry 'Tibbie Shiel's' at St Mary's Loch, was synonymous with good cheer and conviviality. Her customers included William Aytoun, John Wilson ('Christopher North'), Robert Chambers, and James Hogg, 'The Ettrick Shepherd', in whose mother's employ Tibbie served as a girl.

19. A clutch of Border aristocrats, 1879. On the left of the table, Lady Louisa Jane Hamilton, wife of William Henry Walter, 6th Duke of Buccleugh and 8th Duke of Queensberry, entertains her brother and sister-in-law, the Claude Hamiltons. The Earl of Dalkeith is wearing a Tam O'Shanter. Next to his mother sits moodily John Charles, who became the 7th Duke, and across the table his brother George William, who was to become a Lt Colonel. Their mother was Mistress of the Robes to both Queen Victoria and Queen Alexandra.

20. Barefoot urchins in Lauder. Taken, circa 1910, by the 14th Earl of Lauderdale.

21. Gwendoline Lucy, wife of Frederick Colin, 14th Earl of Lauderdale, shortly after their marriage in 1890. The sedan-chairmen were footmen from Thirlestane Castle. Victorian photograph albums reveal a great deal of solemnity and much smiling vapidity, but many incorporate the late-Victorian and early Edwardian love of play-acting and 'dressing-up'.

22. Choir of the East United Free Church, Eyemouth, 1898. Founded in 1841, the congregation of the church lost 27 of their members in the great disaster of 1881 (See: Introduction, p12). Their minister, David Kinloch Miller, worked hard to comfort the stricken families.

The people in the photograph represent some of the oldest Eyemouth names:

Back Row: J. Scott, J. Cairnie, J. Burgon.

3rd Row: D. Walker, J. Fairbairn, Miss Sanderson, A. Gillie.

2nd Row: W. Angus, J. Burgon, T. Swanston, K. Miller, G. Middlemass.

Front Row: J. Fairbairn, H. Gillie, I. Fairbairn, J. Miller.

23. The Head Gardner and his staff of 22 *en fête*, at the home of the Earl of Home; The Hirsel, Coldstream, Berwickshire, 1870.

24. A visit to the smallest cemetery in Scotland, at Galashiels, 1880s.

25. Pupils of Bowhill School, near Newark Tower, Yarrow valley, circa 1900. This school was on the estate of the Duke of Buccleugh, and was maintained in books by him until taken over by the County Education Authority. The children are unusually well-dressed for the period and the class, although the faces are tinged with hardship and the boredom of the classroom. Border schools began each morning with a hymn, a prayer and a Bible reading. Much elementary learning, following the 1870 Elementary Education Act, was drearily factual and repetitive in method. School photographs are rare before 1890.

CHAPTER TWO

HOW WAGES WERE EARNED

ONE obvious characteristic of the maturing Border industrial society was the contraction of the agricultural labour force. The decline of agriculture as the main source of wage-earning in the Borders was an inevitability after the developing of the industrial revolution of the late 1780s. Rural workers were understandably attracted by the higher wages to be earned in factories. As the agricultural depression of the 1870s to 1900s bit, departure from the land was quickened.

In the central Borders, textiles were the major source of employment for women. They comprised a regular 62 percent of the textile mill workforce right up to the 1900s. On the average they earned a half to two-thirds the wages of their male counterparts. Women in the mills had an important place because they were alleged to cope better with the harsh and remitting discipline of factory work than men. Indeed the use of women in the textile mills was only a continuation of the traditional family employment in clothing manufacture that pre-dated the industrial revolution.

By the 1870s many town and country women were employed in domestic service. It is interesting to note that a precise hierarchy existed among the 'living in' servants. Teenage girls usually occupied the kitchen, and graduated to being nursery maids and laundry maids, thence to parlour maids and on to the dizzy heights of cook and housekeeper. Domestic service expanded in the Borders from the early 1880s as the middle class widened by commercial expansion.

This was the age of coal and steam, as the textile mills, the forges and the railways were thus fuelled. So the number of people employed to handle coal were legion. In the Borders coalmen's drays were a common sight and the itinerant coal shoveller earned a steady, if low, remuneration.

In the less well regulated, and predominantly workshop trades, it was still possible to work a 12 hour day, even up to 1900; but the average was 60 hours per week (in the 1870s, say) in the Borders. By 1870 no child could work under the age of 8; and, from 8—13 a maximum working day of 6½ hours was proscribed by at least 10 hours a week compulsory education.

Wages varied enormously in the Border trades, but unskilled and semi-skilled workers, by the 1890s, were earning 18s—30s (£0.90—£1.50) per week. With overtime a skilled man could earn £2 a week by 1900. Agricultural workers had one advantage over the town labourer in that there were 'perks' of edibles from the land.

Still in Victorian and Edwardian times, as these pictures show, there was room for the craftsman worker, from blacksmith to wheelwright and from monumental mason to farrier, carpenter and gravestone cutter.

26. Bondagers at Cornhill-on-Tweed, Northumberland. Left to Right they are: B. Johnston; L. Wastle, K. Wastle (sisters); A. Fraser; L. Hope; E. Fraser; K. Hope.

27. Bondagers at Melrose, circa 1900. Every hind, horsekeeper or farm worker was expected to find a 'bondager'—a woman
to work for as long as an employer required—as part of a hiring agreement. Usually the bondagers were daughters, sisters
or spinster relatives of a farm worker. By 1912, they could earn 2s (10p) a day. They were known for their distinctive
dress or poke-bonnet and blue 'ugly', which gave way to a brown straw hat with turndown brim, and a pink scarf to secure
the hat. A blue blouse, thick woollen stockings and hob-nail books completed the garb.

28. A binding and stooking team of three men and two horses at Broughton Knowe, Peebles, circa 1900. Such teams were common throughout the Borders.

29. Village wheelwright, Darnick, Roxburghshire, circa 1880. Note the 'river bed' stonework of the houses, the thatched roofs and the oil streetlamp.

30. Jessie Scott from High Blantyre, who worked at Cowbog Farm, Morebattle, Roxburghshire, circa 1902, tends her cow. She is holding a 'luggie', which was placed between the milker's knees to collect the milk; this cow is obviously a 'good milker' as a large metal pail is needed too.

31. The village blacksmith at Blainslie, Galashiels, shoes a workhorse, circa 1909.

32. Here a farmer has taken over a farm outside Selkirk and is receiving traditional help from his neighbours. They have brought men and equipment to give 'a day's ploughing'. In many cases it was a social occasion rather than hard work; note the whisky, and the 'dressy' harnesses.

33. William Falla, blacksmith, Lilliesleaf, Roxburghshire. An essential village craftsman while the horse held sway, the blacksmith was usually a source of much local information. His forge offered opportunities not only to make horseshoes, but also agricultural implements. Blacksmiths' shops often descended from father to son; such businesses crumbled before the power of the combustion engine.

34. Tom Scott, blacksmith and wheelwright, circa 1895. He volunteered for the Boer War, and was killed in action in World War I.

35. The first horse-drawn fire engine at Peebles, 1911.

36. Hawick Fire Brigade at practice outside Wilton Lodge, Hawick, 1899. After 1910, motorised Leyland fire engines were popular with brigades.

◆
37.
Melrose 11-man Fire Engine
with tender, circa 1890.

◆
38.
John Fairbairn, circa 1880,
gravestone sculptor who is said
to have worked in every
graveyard in the Borders.
He is buried in Melrose Abbey
graveyard surrounded by his
handiwork.

39. Interior of Hawick Co-operative Store, built in 1885 and opened 1886 by Mr Maxwell of the SCWS.

40. Robert Oliphant with fellow workers at the grocery shop in Bridge Street, Hawick, 1908. Multiply the prices by eight to arrive at modern spending power.

41. A grimy, grim-faced Berwickshire sweep poses circa 1890.

42. Two pretty Salvation Army Officers, Selkirk, 1888. Salvationists were at work in Selkirk by 1883.

43. Alex. Stainton, Hawick town bellringer and crier. He was a stocking maker by trade.

44. Tammie Thomson, a Galashiels postman, 1908. He has six service stripes, one for each five years of service: 1 s (5 p) extra wage was paid for every stripe.

45. A Hawick laundry ironing room at the turn of the century. Laundry work was badly paid and very time consuming. The Victorian and Edwardian predilection for lace meant a boom time in 1890-1907 for elaborate dresses and curtains. All these had to be hand ironed (notice the gas irons on the centre table) and carefully hung; the bassinet cover (on the left) would call for much tedious ironing.

46. Steeplejacks employed by Robert Hall & Co, Galashiels, scale the chimney of the Bridge Mill, 1908. The mill was built in 1818 and was known as Huddersfield Mill until 1907 when Peter Anderson, the new owner, changed the name.

47. A road gang repairing Buccleuch Rd, Selkirk, 1890. Note the boy with the (red) flag—a necessity for all road engines until 1896.

48. Alexander Purves (first on the left) and the Gordon raspberry pickers, Berwickshire. The land was owned by Henderson of Fawside Lodge who planted the berries for the benefit of Gordon folk; they picked their own and paid him so much per pound.

49. The Selkirk Rifle Volunteers (members of the KOSBs), who sailed from Southampton, 14th February 1900, bound for the South African Campaign (Boer War 1899-1902).

50. 'Open day' at the Border hill training camp of the Border Rifle Volunteers, circa 1903.

51. The counting and packing department of Young Trotter & Son Ltd, papermakers, Chirnside Bridge, Berwickshire, circa 1899. Established 1786 at Broomhouse, Duns, the mill was transferred to Chirnside in 1842. Papermaking was strictly a Berwickshire manufacturing phenomenon in the Borders with mills also at Ayton and Edington Hill (wrapping paper).

52. A fisherman on the quay of 1892-93, Eyemouth, Berwickshire. 17th century Gunsgreen House and turreted battlement, once the haunt of smugglers, lies across the water.

53.
Fishing smack at
St Abb's Head
anchorage,
circa 1900.
Fishermen 'pole' the
boat to shore.

54. Eyemouth harbour entrance, which was re-opened after improvements in 1885 by Lady Tweedmouth.

55. The *James Gillie* lies at anchor at Eyemouth, circa 1890. St John's church towers above the skyline.

56. Seahouses Lifeboat, Northumberland. The 14-man crew turn out for a life-jacket drill.

57. The fish gutters of Eyemouth take a break. These girls travelled up and down the coast following the catches.

58. Mr Currie the sculptor working in his yard in the shadow of Darnick's tower of 1569. A bust of Robert Burns stares blankly at the camera.

59. John Watson and his coal cart block a Peebles road. When this picture was taken in 1888, John was selling his coal for 9s (45p) a TON!

60. Henderson's Post Office at Gavinton, Berwickshire, Circa 1890. Most of the houses at that time were owned by the Langton Estate.

61. The clogmaker of Newcastleton, on the Liddle Water, Roxburghshire. A few Border quarrymen, coalmen, roadmenders, sweeps and scaffies still wore clogs in the late 1890s.

62. The Head Gardner instructs his staff at the Hirsel, Coldstream, 1880. A garden staff of 20—30 was not uncommon on the larger Border estates.

63. 'Coal Jean' and 'Coal Geordie', Peebles, 1880. This couple followed the coal carts and carried the coal to customers' homes (sometimes a long way from the road), for delivery men just dumped coal in the road outside a house. The couple existed on tips so earned.

64. Simon Paterson, Melrose bellman, had a nose of noteworthy size and colour, circa 1870.

65. Lizzie Dickson was at one time the only female 'post
runner' in Scotland. The photograph was taken in Melrose,
circa 1890.

67. James Rennie the last town drummer of Peebles; he also
    'cried' the wares of local shopkeepers. 1899.

66. Annie Stone, Jessie McIntosh and Mary Murray, nurse-
    maids to professional people in Morebattle. Here they
    care for their small charges by the Kale water on More-
    battle Tofts; Grubbet Law is in the background.

68. Estate workers in their Sunday best foregather at Philiphaugh House, Selkirk, 24th July 1903.

69. 'Loosin' time at a Border factory, circa 1900. The 'bunnet' was a mark of the mature workingman, and it was unusual to see bareheaded workers over 16 years of age.

70. Hawick Cooperative Storeman delivering supplies to William Reid of the Buccleuch Temperance Hotel, Hawick, 1882. Note the uncovered trays of bread on the van roof.

71. Workers, family and delivery boys at William Curle's bakery door, Duns, 1900.

CHAPTER THREE

THE TEXTILE INDUSTRY

THE rise of heavy industry during the early years of Victoria's reign to 1870 was a godsend for the Border textile manufacturers. During this period a highly efficient woollen textile industry, specialising in the production of tweeds, was built up in the Borders, principally at Hawick, Galashiels and Innerleithen. This had offset the intense competition from Lancashire that had had a detrimental effect on the Border handloom weavers; by 1837 a Border handloom weaver was earning as little as 4/- (20p) per week.

Urban expansion in the Borders was distinctly linked to the textile trade, although the area had been from monastic times a major producer of wool and cloth. The growth of Innerleithen, for instance, had been stimulated by Alex Brodie, a local blacksmith who had made his fortune in the Shropshire iron-rade, when he built a five-story woollen mill in the 1780s. Because of the textile industry the population of Hawick increased fourfold during 1801-61, a reflection of the great impetus gained by the burgh's functional change. Indeed, the water-powered woollen mills had led to the creation of new villages, like Walkerburn and Earlston. By the late 1790s, of course a woollen manufactory had been established at Peebles.

By 1837, the Border towns, particularly Galashiels, led Britain in the range of processes which had been successfully mechanised. There was a flexibility of mind among Border manufacturers to adopt new inventions and this was the foundation of the success of Border entrepreneurs, which was taken to its height by the introduction of tweeds. During the period of this book alone, Galashiels saw the establishment of five woollen spinning mills: Abbots (1841), Buckholm (1846), Comeleybank (1852), Tweed (1852), and Victoria (1853).

This was to have an important effect on the guarantee of employment where wages were as good as anywhere. Yet, while agricultural wages rose in 1900-1910, for instance, by 15%, the subsequent recessions in heavy industry only produced an increase of 1% among textile workers.

Hawick, by way of example, saw strong workingclass movements for home ownership and because of the textile industry, from the 1870s, the workingclass who owned their own homes did so out of accumulated savings. To keep one jump ahead of them, the middle class raised loans by mortgage, supported by regular salaries from textile manufacturing.

Yet, by and large the quality of workmanship in many of the workingclass houses was poor, as is witnessed in the Borders jingle about plumbers:

> I scamp the joints, I scamp the drains,
> I am an artful plumber;
> You'll feel my hand in winter's rains,
> You'll sniff it in the summer.

Alas, too, because of the expansion of textiles, pollution was brought to the Borders. By the 1870s the Tweed was acting as a sewer for Galashiels, Peebles and Innerleithen.

72.   Hand knitting machine, with boy at the winding wheel, at Peter Scott's hosiery factory, Hawick,1889.

73. Miss Fanny Dunn of Dod Mill, Lauder, 1910.
Her spinning wheel dated from the early 1800s.

74. Warper at work in a Selkirk Mill, circa 1900.

75. Darning Department at Gibson & Lumga
Ltd's mill of St Mary's Selkirk, circa 1900

76.   Working at the broad handframe and the winding wheel in John Laing & Son's hosiery mill, Hawick, circa 1910.

77.   Knitting frame at John Laing & Sons, Hawick, circa 1910.

78. A typical millhouse for the wet finishing of the cloth. A hydro-extraction stitching machine is on the right. Note the dry pairs of boots under the table. Robert Noble's mill, Hawick.

79. Shows apprentices attending a twinning frame at Robert Noble's, Hawick. The most common garb of such workers was knickerbockers and long aprons.

80. Part of the 40-loom shed at Robert Noble's, Hawick, circa 1900. Such looms were lit by gas jets above.

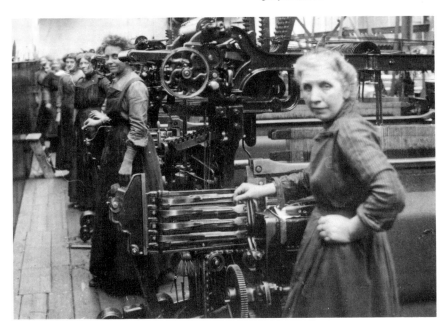

81. Boys working winding machines in the mill of John Laing & Sons, Hawick, circa 1910.

CHAPTER FOUR

SCENES AND MEMORIES LONG FORGOTTEN

AMONG these fading photographs the reader and social historian can glimpse fragments of the lives of the folk of the Borders. Herein a hundred isolated moments can be touched, and we can reach down the years to hear the echoes of voices long still, grasp the meaning of day-to-day Border life and take in the scenery in which it was enacted.

Victorian Border towns were at once both pride and perturbation to their creators and administrators. Yet, their presence in all their profusion and diversity, was a tribute in brick and stone to the Border man of commerce and craft. By the 1880s no less than 80 per cent of Borderers lived in towns and villages. Civic leaders took enormous pride in their creations, and never ducked the 'responsibility' of adding their surnames to a landmark. Libraries and public gardens were added by the Edwardians for the mental and aesthetic hungers of the electorate. Town Halls were refurbished on a grand scale, and shop fronts and offices gave splendid scope for the architectural imagination. But some artifacts of the years before Victoria were retained, like Mercat Crosses, and were enshrined in Gothic to last for evermore.

Money wages doubled between 1850 and 1910, bringing obvious benefits to those workers, predominantly skilled, who were able to bargain with their employers for a larger share of industrial prosperity. By and large the workingclass spent nearly all their earnings on basic foods. So their clothes in these pictures always look more careworn than those of their masters. Foodshops in the Border towns reflected the popularity of foods rich in carbo-hydrates for energy, but low on protein and vitamins; coarse bread was eaten more than meat and potatoes soared above fruit and vegetable sales. Even so, as these pictures show, the odd luxury of perambulator, or bicycle was afforded.

82.
Lindean Station, on the
Galashiels—Selkirk Line,
circa 1890.

83. The old Town Hall of Hawick, built in 1781 for £300 in place of the earlier tolbooth and jail. It was demolished in 1884, when the present building was commenced.

84. The Lawson footbridge across the Teviot at Hawick, 1886. Bailie Alexander S. Lawson (1864-1910)—after whom the bridge is named—is in the centre of the three figures.

85. Hawick 1910. By 1511 the town was a Burgh of Barony, which meant it was empowered to have its own market and fairs by right of the Crown. Pedestrians are unimpeded by traffic.

86.   A delightful, busy, thoughtfully posed picture of a Hawick thoroughfare, circa 1880.

87.   Selkirk Market Place, circa 1910, outside County Motors. The cows and trap are relics of a slower, pastoral society.

88. The Market Place, Selkirk, after the severe weather of March 1880. Selkirk, a Royal Burgh founded in 1328, has always been proud of its heritage. Sir Walter Scott looks down benignly on snowballing Soutars.

89. A family poses outside the Fleece Hotel, Selkirk, around 1900. Then, people had time to stand and stare, soon their quiet lifestyle was to be shattered for ever by World War I.

90. Newtown St. Boswells circa 1900.

91. A line of Sundayschool children form up to await their transport at Easter Street, Duns, circa 1900. Sundayschool outings were very popular in Victorian and Edwardian times.

92. Hens scratch and children play 'bools' in the dust outside a thatched cottage in the village of Midlem, near Bowden, Roxburghshire, circa 1900.

93. The Square and Town Hall, Duns, Berwickshire, 1900. This piece of Victorian gothic has been swept away and the shop fronts altered.

94. A rare Old Gala Club print showing the tall chimney of the Corn Mill (known as the 'Auld Mill'), demolished in 1909. On the left of the tree in the centre of the picture is the old Miller's house, demolished in 1909. Founded in 1599 as a Burgh of Barony, Galashiels can trace its heritage back to the time when it was only a village of wooden huts, or 'sheils' beside the Gala Water.

95. High Street, Galashiels, circa 1900. A photographer setting up his equipment was a magnet for street urchins, knickerbockered delivery boys and auld wifies peering round the chintz curtains. Yet, the photographer who gave us this picture has left more than an array of the curious. Here gaslamp standards, lamps with leaded lights, delivery vans and large mural adverts vie for attention. Among the shops shown here there was a stability of tenancy because of the strength of the textile trade at this time.

96.   Bank St, Galashiels, on a summer's day at the turn of the century. Notice the allotments on the right hand side of the street. The blue slated roofs were a feature of the town.

97.   Laying the sewers in St Andrew Street, Galashiels, 1908. All such work was labour intensive with no mechanical diggers.

98.   The Auld Corn Mill in Galashiels, demolished in 1909. It was removed to make way for the fountain designed
by Sir Robert Lorimer, now part of the town centre.

99.   Abbotsford House, from the River Tweed, the home of Sir Walter Scott. Scott bought the property from the
Rev. Dr. Douglas in 1811 for 4000 guineas. Its ultimate opulence crippled him financially.

100. The sawmill at Mossburnford, near Jedburgh, circa 1880, when it was run by the Hislop family. The old name for the buildings was Gundy's Neuk. In the foreground, beyond the logs is a tricycle popular at the time. A similar tricycle set up a record in the early 1890s when W.F. Sutton rode from London to Edinburgh in 2 days 9 hours.

101. A saunter in Denholm Dean, on the Cavers estate, near Hawick, circa 1890. The building on the left is a caretaker's residence; she ran the tearoom on the right for the benefit of the laird's wife.

102. The Auld Mid Row, Hawick, 1881; it was demolished in 1884. The photograph was taken from the foot of the Loan near the entrance to the Poor House, later incorporated into Drumlanrig Hospital. Note the well in the foreground which once stood outside a blacksmith's shop.

103. A gig outside the smithy cottage, Allanton, Berwickshire. Up to the early 1920s, the village was owned by the Houston-Boswalls of nearby Blackadder House.

104. The High St and Marygate, leading to the Scotsgate, Berwick-on-Tweed, Northumberland, in 1876. The stalls are set out to sell fish and vegetables. Although some carts pass along, pedestrians can still hold conversations in the middle of the road in perfect safety. Nor is the horse-drawn gig an inconvenience as it makes its way down the still cobbled street. Marygate was one of the finest high streets in England, and many of the houses seen here date from the rebuilding of 1754.

105. High St, Berwick-on-Tweed, circa 1900. The Town Hall was started in 1750 and completed in 1761. The Red Lion Inn on the right was an important coaching inn of the 18th—19th centuries.

106. St Abb's harbour, 1908, built by a member of the brewing family of Usher, who stipulated that there should be no public house in the little fishing village!

107. Fishing cobbles on the banks of the River Tweed, in the shadow of the Elizabethan walls, Berwick-on-Tweed. Started in 1611 the bridge was completed in 1634. The sixth pier with the heightened parapet formerly marked the boundary between Berwick and North Durham. Tweedmouth lies to the south of the bridge.

108. A girl poses at Hounam, 11 miles from Kelso; a village with a Highland aspect.

109. Picnicers gather on the banks of the Tweed for St James's Fair, Kelso, 1910. Note the wooden bridge put up especially for the fair; it cost one penny to cross.

110. Kelso market place on the morning after St James Fair, 6th August 1886. The tinks and showmen prepare to move out.

111. Lauder, the only royal Burgh in Berwickshire, on a quiet Sunday afternoon in 1902. The Sunday stroll was a must for Borderfolk.

112. Earlston Square, Berwickshire, 1905. The girl's sporting bicycles would be a source of envy to their pals.

113. The 12th century Cistercian Abbey of Melrose, looking towards the great east window, surmounted by the
great tower of 14th—15th century. The Abbey Hotel and the Custodian's House have been removed, and stood
on the site of the Abbey narthex.

114-115.

A day for sheep and a day for goats outside the Station Hotel, Market Square, Melrose, 1905. The Mercat Cross bears the date 1645 and was re-set here in 1842.

116. Melrose Parish Church, built in 1810 by Messrs Smith of Darnick, who rebuilt the Mercat Cross. The tower survived the fire of 1908.

117. The Edinburgh Border Counties Association take over Leyden's cottage at Denholm, 28th July 1896. On the green at Denholm an obelisk was set up in 1861 to the memory of the village's most famous scholar John Leyden (1775-1811). Self-educated, Leyden became a reviewer for the *Edinburgh Magazine*, was a friend of Sir Walter Scott and travelled to India. He was to become one of the most distinguished Orientalists of his day.

118. Peebles High Street, described as 'the most handsome in the Borders'. Flanked by a quartet of lampstandards and the inevitable urchins, the Mercat Cross was set here on a modern base in 1895.

119.
The popular Tweedside walk at Peebles, looking towards the Town Bridge, 1910, widened in 1900. On the left is the tall crocketed lantern spire of the 18th century parish church.

120. The secluded village of Lilliesleaf, by the Ale Water, had a church here in the 12th century. For 700 years the village was dominated by the Riddells of Riddell who went bankrupt in 1819, their estates dwindling. Yet there was still Riddell property around in the era of this book. The cottage in the distance with the mural lattice work belonged to the Riddell estate, whose cottages all had this feature. The gig stands outside the Cross Keys Inn, with its lintle lamp.

CHAPTER FIVE

TRAVEL AND TRANSPORT

THE golden age of early photography saw the development of mass public transport. In particular it was the era of travel by rail. It was the influence of the railway, more than anything else, that gave the ordinary Victorian Borderer his first real taste of mobility. Even so, by the late 1870s there were still those who had not been beyond their parish boundaries in the longest lifetime. Remote termini and railway junctions generated sufficient employment for new settlements to be created. Indeed, before the coming of the North British Railway, Riccarton, Roxburghshire was a bare hillside a goodly distance from a main road. After Riccarton station was built a whole railway community was built to service trains of the Waverley route in their passage through the Border Hills. Peebles (1853) and Jedburgh (1852), for instance, obtained their railways along the line of engineer Thomas Bouch's 'St Andrews scheme' (1852), which had been encouraged by Major H.L. Playfair, the progressive Provost.

While Britain invented railways, the symbol of the 19th century, the corresponding mark of the 20th century, the motor car, resulted from experiments in France, Germany and the United States. The first car, a Benz, was imported into Britain in 1894, and with it the hobby of motoring was invented. By 1896 so important a political lobby has been set up by motorists that the Locomotives on Highways Act was passed; this removed many of the restrictions on road transport imposed by the notorious 'Red Flag Act' (a man had to walk ahead of a motor car with a warning red flag). Now Border motorists could whiz along the road at 14 mph! Seeing mass transit potential, the Scots were the first to inaugurate a motor 'bus service in 1898 in Edinburgh, and the Borders were 'opened up' thereafter by private-hire omnibuses. By 1905 the Borders witnessed a 'boom' in 'bus trips.

Health-giving, hygienic, gateway to the countryside and freedom—away from all the chafing narrowness of Victorian home-life on a non-chafing saddle at a guinea each—was the promise of the development of cycling. Like H.G. Wells' hero-clerk, Mr Polly in 1910, cycling realised the dreams of many Border travellers. Yet, cycling did more socially for Border women than Border men. For many middle-class women cycling became a mark of emancipation, and there were those who not only used their cycles for leisure and exercise, but also used them to get to work. So employers (and schools) had to build new cycle sheds.

Nevertheless in the larger period of this book the over-riding theme of Border transport, commercial and leisure, was horse-driven. Coal men, milk men, brewers' draymen all delivered by horse; and the first omnibuses were pulled by horses. Even the railways themselves were served by horse cabs and delivery vans. Even by the late 1890s in the Borders, one horse for every ten people was needed to keep society going.

121. A Hawick man of the 1890s sports his cycle-suit and poses in a studio for an 'action print'. Such cruiser tricycles became popular after being ridden by H.R.H. The Prince of Wales, and H.R.H. Princess Mary Adelaide, Duchess of Teck.

122. Members of a Hawick Touring Club on their 1890 machine. Although introduced in the 1860s it was the invention of the pneumatic tyre in the 1890s which gave impetus to a cycling craze.

123. Gig meets Pennyfarthing cycle. The photograph was taken near Mansfield Gasworks, Hawick, 1890. Ex-cornet Taylor holds the bicycle.

124. Yarn being unloaded at Peter Scott's 'Pesco' Hosiery Factory, Buccleuch Street, Hawick, 1904.

125. Elizabeth and Ada Home with their groom and carriage at the Hirsel, Coldstream, 1869.

126. Most upper-middle class children had their own miniature carriages. Here Margaret, Beatrix and Issobel Douglas-Home drive their dray at Branksome Dene in 1892. 'Mousie' and 'Daisy' are between the shafts.

127. A selection of conveyances outside the 'Gordon Arms' in the Yarrow Valley, near St Mary's Loch, c1889. The smell of drying horse dung perfumed the streets of town and village in summer. Possession of horse-drawn transportation was a mark of social status. The horse also gave much employment to coachmen, grooms and stable staff. There was work too for an army of road sweepers and a permanent hygiene headache.

128. Engine No 661 of the North British Railway Co, Hawick Station 1891. Rail trips to Edinburgh were all the rage at this time and were the inspiration for the hilarious Border 'best-seller' 'Betty's Trip Tae Edinbury' written by the 'Black Spider': this was the pen-name of Alex Purves, the henpecked owner of the 'Imperial Hotel', Hawick. According to Purves's book 'A third class ticket tae Edinbury' cost 3/9½d (return) or 19p.

129.

130. Leaderfoot Viaduct.

131.
Engine 487 arrives
from Edinburgh at
the North British
(later L.N.E.R.)
station, Peebles.

132.
Viaduct Bridge over
the Tweed, near
Peebles, on the LMS
branch line to
Glasgow. The train is
emerging from
South Park Tunnel.
This line was the
work of Scott the
contractors of
Kilmarnock, 1863.

133. The paddlesteamer 'Susan' plying the Tweed at Berwick-on-Tweed. Skipper Tommy Elliot is in the bow. Berwick was linked by the trans-river ferries with Tweedmouth and Spittal.

134. Hawick Boy Scout Troop with their own 'make it up yourself' handcart, 1910.

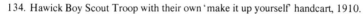

135. A Galashiels party of motorcyclists at St Mary's Loch, with 'bunnets wi' snoots at the back'! They are riding Triumphs, a Douglas and a BSA. Left to Right are: Thomas White, Robert White, James Church, Robert Herberson, James Beggs, and Archibald Inglis.

136. A family of motorcycle enthusiasts at Walter Baxter's shed behind Scott Street, Galashiels, 1908.

137. Thought to be the first hiring car in the Borders, owned by Adam Purves & Sons, Galashiels. The 8hp 'Argyle' is at St Mary's Loch, 1908.

138. Assorted transport in the High Street, Berwick-on-Tweed. Cabs were parked outside the Town Hall, but one seems 'horseless' near to the end of West Street.

139.
Lady Thirlestane at the
wheel. She was the future
wife of the 15th Earl of
Lauderdale (she became
Countess in 1932).
Panhards, Daimlers and
Lanchesters all became the
'rich man's bicycles' after
H.R.H. The Prince of
Wales took up motoring.
By 1898 there were the
first motor races.

140.
A family outing by the
Tweed at Melrose. Note
the ornate perambulator.
Although baby carriages
had appeared in Britain in
the 18th century, by the
mid-Victorian years they
were widespread.

141. Drumlanrig Square, Hawick, typical of the quiet Victorian cobbled backwater. The horse held by the boy is about to be put in the shafts of the carriage.

142.
The pride of ownership is evident in this photograph of circa 1900. An early Selkirkshire registration, LS102, takes members of the Brydon family on an outing. The permitted speed for cars was raised to 20mph in 1904 when number plates became compulsory.

CHAPTER SIX

SOCIAL OCCASIONS

LOOKING through the albums of Victorian and Edwardian Borderers, social occasions are varied. Yet, apart from the other noteworthy events pictured here, the overwhelming number of extant photographs cover five main subjects: Common Riding; picnics; fairs; circuses, and weddings.

The tiny Border burghs were continually the first places to feel the onslaught of the English invaders. Still they celebrate their continuing existence every summer with the flamboyant Common Ridings. Such ridings have had a number of origins. At Hawick, in June, remembrance of the band of youths who scored a victory over English soldiers at Hornshole in 1514 is enacted; in Galashiels a similar event is found in the Braw Lad's Gathering. Although the ridings may have had a pagan origin, an act of more civic than religious tone made the Common Ridings a necessity, when burgh boundaries had to be confirmed each year by riding along their length. Berwick-on-Tweed is the only English Border town to have such ridings.

The picnic was an important part of the Victorian and Edwardian leisure time, most on a grand scale organised by firm and Sundayschool. Much labour went into preparations, both of food and gaily decorated carts to take the picnickers to their destinations. As the foreign church missionaries wooed the natives with bangles and beads, their Border counterparts touted for custom in the magnificence of their picnics.

Fairs have been comon occurrences in the Borders since medieval times when both the church and the crown gave rights to hold fairs; usually attached to markets. They had begun as commercial gatherings for the sale of livestock, but by the 1830s were well established as social gatherings attracting entertainers of all kinds. Fairground amusements were revolutionised in the 1860s with the use of steam power, and again in the 1880s with the introduction of electricity. It was from this decade that the still familiar amusements, from roundabouts to ferris wheels, date.

Following the Parisian entrepreneurs and the shows of C. Phineas Taylor Barnum (1810-91) and William Frederick Cody (Buffalo Bill, 1846-1917) circuses toured the Border towns regularly from the late 1880s. From time to time chained negroes were brought to the town as 'wild men' and dancing bears were popular in the 1890s. It was the circus proprietors like Ginett who brought such (music hall) acts as the flying trapeze, the wire walkers and the 'Human Cannonballs' to the Borders.

Festivity or woe brought the Victorian and Edwardian family together. Nothing was enjoyed more than 'the good greet' of the funeral (especially after the untimely death of the Prince Consort in 1861 which gave undertakers the excuse to dramatise their wares) or a wedding; although the wedding photographs of yesteryear show a constipated lifelessness around the sitters rather than joy.

Yet, perhaps the dour men of the wedding party were contemplating the emergence of the 'new woman'. Women themselves were fast destroying their 'mystery' by 1900, by smoking, bridge, tennis and knickerbocker cycling. The Victorian prude was giving way to the Edwardian hoyden as women squared up to the militancy of the Votes for Women campaign.

143. John Douglas, known as 'Douglas the Brave', photographed when he was 82. Douglas 'Cast the
Colours' of the Selkirk Incorporation of Hammermen at the Selkirk Common Riding every year from
1831-85. The honour of 'casting' the flag usually changed from person to person every year.

144. Cornet Andrew Leyden, with his 'Right-hand Man' Andrew Knox, and his 'Left-hand Man' John Elliot at Hawick's Common Riding, 1857.

145. The dining Marquee of the Galashiels Boy's Brigade Camp, Gosford, Northumberland, 1911. Founded in 1883, the aim of the brigade was 'the advancement of Christ's Kingdom amongst boys and the promotion of habits of obedience, reverence, discipline, self-respect and all that tends towards true Christian manliness'.

146. Gala Cycling Club hold their annual camp at Spittal; Berwick-on-Tweed is in the background.

147. The United Sunday Schools of Jedburgh, headed by the Boy's Brigade Band, parade through the Market Place en route for the annual picnic, 1895.

148. Gala Harrriers Sports Fête, 29th July 1908.

149. Children from Chirnside, Berwickshire, make their way to a picnic at Coldingham Beach, 1905.

150. Dancing at the Common Riding celebrations on the Hawick Moor, circa 1900.

151. Held annually since 1853, the Jedburgh 'Border Games' take place in Lothian Park, beside the abbey. Many of Scotland's professional athletes have competed here for prize money. Circa 1890.

152. Presentation of medal to soldier from the Selkirk area who served in the South African War. Presentation being made by Miss Craig-Brown and Provost James Russell. September 1902.

153. The opening of the Masonic Bazaar in Hawick Town Hall, 15th Sept 1887.

154. Crowning the Beltane Queen, Peebles. This ceremony usually takes place in the third week in June. Common Riding was resuscitated in 1897 in Peebles to commemorate Queen Victoria's Diamond Jubilee.

155. The travelling circus moves from Melrose to Galashiels. Photograph taken on Melrose Road, Galashiels.

156. Gala Band at the Fall of Clyde. First Liberal Party 'Trip', 1905.

157. The bride arrives at a society wedding in Duns, Berwickshire, circa 1900. Police Inspector Joseph Young is on duty by the right of the door.

158. Outing to 'The Glen', Peebles, by Veitch's Drapery and Dressmaking staff, 1895. Robert Veitch, the firms founder is in the centre of the middle row. Established in 1884, Veitch's corner was a trysting place for Peebles youth.

159. Flower bedecked wedding party of Robert S. Muir, Heather Bank Mills, Selkirk. He married Miss Alice Carnegie Alexander of Upland. 4th June 1908.

CHAPTER SEVEN

LEISURE AND SPORT

DURING the years 1870 to 1900 the Borders saw the creation of the mass entertainment industry, as a consequence of the revolution in technological developments. This too was boosted by the reorganisation of work times and the introduction of 'days off' and 'half days'. First came the Saturday half-holiday, then early closing days, and a feature of Border commercial life 'the monthly holiday' which often meant a trip to Edinburgh. The 1871 Bank Holiday Act led to the company holidays, first without and then with pay. As prices fell from the 1870s, more people had more money to spend on their new-found leisure.

In workingclass areas the public house was the first institution to benefit from the better funded leisure; and, the middle classes, forsworn the 'pub' for class reasons, engendered the development of the eating house where ladies could be taken. In the wake of the leisure time drinkers came the do-gooders of the temperance movement whose intentions publicly ranged against alcoholic beverages, but who were fundamentally concerned with what people actually decided to do with their leisure as an alternative.

During the 1890s a clutch of new inventions, from the cinema to the gramophone, heralded new leisure pursuits, but, by and large Border folk pursued the 'New Athleticism' which had come out of the 1860s and chose 'physical leisure'. Probably because of the Calvinist-Liberal traditions of the Border Counties, people saw sport as not only a promoter of physical fitness, but a moulder of character and self-discipline. One interesting factor in the Borders is that sport broke down class barriers more than anything else. Music, however, remained strictly 'highbrow' (Sir Edward Elgar to Mozart) or 'lowbrow' (music hall)—even in prayer the classes remained divided with the workingclass bellowing out their Sankey hymns, and the middle class intoning (with as much enthusiasm as was decorous on a Sunday) such hymns as the 'Onward Christian Soldiers' of Sir Arthur Sullivan.

Fishing, curling, running, swimming, cricket, rugby, walking, outings to the seaside and football were all followed with equal verve in the Borders, and became organised with rules and regulations like those which evolved from the establishment of the Football League in 1888. Golf, of course, having many of its birthpangs in Scotland, developed more of a mass appeal when King Edward took it up. Golf developed as a spectator sport in earnest, when such as former Prime Minister Arthur Balfour played against the former champion Harry Vardon in 1908. Boxing, by and large, was considered a disreputable sport in Edwardian times.

The face of sport was entirely changed when women entered the lists as curlers, ice-hockey players and even footballers with a difference: The Edwardian craze for roller skates led to women playing football on them!

160. The Tweed at the 'Three Stanes' Beat, 1870, Coldstream.

161. Spoofing a salmon catch at the Hirsel, Coldstream, circa 1900.

162. Match between James Braid, Open Champion 1901 and Harry Vandon, Open Champion, 1896, 1898, 1899, over 36 holes, on 25th Sept 1901, at Vertish Hill, Hawick Golf Course.

163. Hawick Cycling Club, 1889. Note their distinctive cycling suits. The club was established in 1881.

164. Dick Lyon and Alex Stainton about to begin a challenge race at Miller's Knowes, Hawick. Circa 1900. Stainton won.

165. Early Selkirk Cricket Team, 1856. They played on the ground adjacent to the railway station (Engine house in the background). The longest strike in the world was claimed here when a ball landed in an open truck and was carried away to Galashiels!

166. Seven popular rugby players of the Gala Club, 1891. L to r: J. Ward. T. Smart. J. Ford. A. Dalgleish. D.H. Rutherford; A. Smith; R. Murdison.

167. Buccleuch Bowling Club, 1898. L to r: Robert Scoony; T. Lamb; G. Little; and A. Angus.

168. Bert Lawrie, bowler, at Selkirk Bowling Club, Scott's Place, Selkirk. His unusual playing action was due to his false leg.

169. James Curle the famous archaeologist (he excavated the Roman camp at Newstead, near Melrose) curls at Melrose, circa 1900.

170. Melrose Curling Club, circa 1900.

171. Kelso Rifle Club, Mellendean, 1890, under the instruction of Sgt. Instructor Wardle (third from left).

172. Curling Bonspiel at Gattonside, Roxburghshire.

CHAPTER EIGHT

EVENTS

TO

REMEMBER

173. Balloon launched at Martinshouse, Hawick, 1880.

174. A bedecked Cross Keys Hotel, Kelso, with bonfire ready to light on Coronation Day, 9th August 1902.

175. Patriotic banners and flags filled Jedburgh Market Place to celebrate Queen Victoria's Diamond Jubilee, 1897.

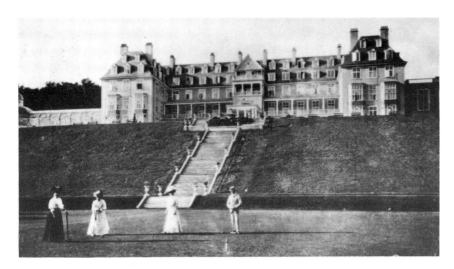

176.
Peebles Hydropathic from
Tennis Green, after the fire.

177.
Peebles Hydro,
burned 7th July 1905.

178.
After the blaze, late 1905.

179. The Gypsy King, Kirk Yetholm. Gypsies were established in Scotland by 1505.
Eventually they were driven into remote places and made their homes at Yetholm
from where they could disappear into the Cheviot Hills if hunted by law officers. In
the 18th century the Bennets of Grubet, who owned Kirk Yetholm built cottages for
them. From here the gypsies hawked their wares. Kirk Yetholm was also the scene of
an education experiment aimed at encouraging the gypsies to settle down. The
sponsor of the scheme was Rev John Baird and the Edinburgh-based Society for the
Reformation of the Gypsies. Gypsy children were thus cared for while their parents
were away hawking; the school met with a certain amount of success.

180. Coronation of Charles Blythe II in 1898 as King of the Gypsies. He was the son of Queen Esther. The coronation was encouraged by Rev. Carrick Miller, largely to promote the village of Kirk Yetholm as a tourist resort. The king, really surnamed Rutherford, used the name of his mother (Esther Faa Blythe) in honour of her being the last Queen of the Gypsies.

181. Opening of Melrose Post Office.

182. Rail crash Galashiels, 1901. There were no fatalities only smashed goods vehicles.

183. Erecting the first telephone wires over the Carter Bar.

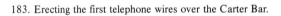